LIFE IS A STORY
WE TELL OURSELVES

Poems, 1992-2012

MARY HIMMELWEIT

Full Court Press
Englewood Cliffs, New Jersey

First Edition

Copyright © 2015 by Mary Himmelweit

All rights reserved. No part of this book may be reproduced or transmitted in any form or by any means electronic or mechanical, including by photocopying, by recording, or by any information storage and retrieval system, without the express permission of the author, except where permitted by law.

Published in the United States of America
by Full Court Press, 601 Palisade Avenue,
Englewood Cliffs, NJ 07632
fullcourtpressnj.com

ISBN 978-1-938812-71-2
Library of Congress Catalog No. 2015958599

Book design by Barry Sheinkopf for Bookshapers.Com
(www.bookshapers.com)

Cover art courtesy of the author

Colophon by Liz Sedlack

ACKNOWLEDGMENTS

Grateful acknowledgment is made to the following publications, in which a number of these poems were previously published:

Medicinal Purposes Literary Review, "My Kid Sister"

The anthology *Songs of Seasoned Women*: "When Was I This Alone With Anyone?"

Poesia: "What He Will Remember"

I am greatly indebted to the late Diana Festa, and the *Madison Poets* writing group, for their advice and encouragement, and to Annette Hollander, Anna Diz, and Ana Doina for their help in the preparation of the manuscript.

TABLE OF CONTENTS

I

Private Reel, 3
All In The Telling, 4
Footprints, 6
In The Beginning There Was The Egg, 7
Fallout, 8
God, Speak To Me, 9
In The Quiet Of Night, 10
Life Measured In Time, 11

II

Scarecrow, 15
Combat, 16
Dominance, 18
In Different Keys, 19
For Centuries, 20
Tsunami, 21
Divination, 22
What Will He Remember, 23
Jump Rope Jingle, 24
Dark Remembrance, 25
Nazi Germany, World War II, 26
Execution, 27

III

Nonpareil, 31
I Fell In Love With A Lion, 32
Wellfleet, 33
Voice Mail, 34
In Two Places At The Same Time, 36
Mars To Venus, 37
Valentine, 38
Yes, 39
Interlude, 40

You Should Have Been There, 41
She Calls Him Honey, 42

IV

Poison Oak, 45
Circus Scene, 46
Ballad, 48
Post-Modernism, 51
Stepmother, 52
Keep Going, 54

V

The Stinging, 57
Father, 58
Drug Resistant, 59
Mother, 60
You Can't Go Home Again, 61
Revelation, 62
When Was I This Alone With Anyone, 63
Kid Sister, 64
Quadrille, 65
Can You Hear Me?, 66
Writer's Block, 67
Time Entrapped, 68

VI

African Good Luck Charm, 71
Etruscan Oil Lamp, 72
Museum, NY, 73
Pierre Bonnard: Large Yellow Nude, 74
"The Hungry God", 75
Avant-Garde, 76
The Color Black, 78
Betrayed, 79
Aperture, 80

VII

Tragicomedy, 83
Moebius-Strip Reality, 84
Alternate Parking Prayer, 86
Encounter, 87
Old-Fashioned Hero, 88
Follow Your Dream, 89
The Rope Arches High, 90
Somewhere, 91
Protector Of The Family, 92

VIII

The Key, 95
Convivencia, 96
Politically Correct In Another Era, 97
The Right To Life And The Pursuit of Happiness, 98
The World In The Palm Of Her Hand, 100
Surfing, 101
Miscast, 102
Mistaken Communion, 103
Goddess Of Beef Cattle, 104
Guest Cabin, 106
End of Season, 107
Irretrievable Losses, 108
Metamorphosis, 109
Subterranean Encounter, 110

IX

Not Yet, 113
The Writing On the Wall, 114
Beguiled, 116
Free Zone, 118
Commemoration, 120
Bringing You Up to Date, 122
Luck, My Heathen God, 123
Alternate Universe, 124

I

PRIVATE REEL

Yesterday, passing a flower shop,
the here and the now dissolved.

Instead, a windblown prairie
under a perfect sky,
buttercups, daisies, wild scallions
dot the meadow,

and I, a six year old, a tiny moist frog
on the palm of my splayed hand,
squeal with delight.

ALL IN THE TELLING

Fifty-five years later I descend from the sky.
My cousin leads me by the hand through the city,
drives me out of town, to my childhood house.

I throw my arms around each linden tree
leading to the house.
Remember me? I'm back!

I have come back!
I listen for the traffic of bumblebees,
butterflies, wasps, and search for the orchard

of apple, pear, and cherry trees,
and on top of the hill, sheltered by oak,
birch, and chestnut trees, the gazebo.

I walk to the pond behind the house—
the water thick, the color of tar,
no yellow-billed ducks in formation.

Spread out on the muddy embankment,
a woman lies dreaming in the rays
of the summer-night sun.

The woman sits up. Our eyes meet.
Behind her, instead of the orchard
half a century of soggy devastation.

Her dream is my memory.
I smile and walk on.

FOOTPRINTS

One day,
my aunt surprised me with a photo.
My cousin Fred and I sit side by side,
young, elegantly dressed.

Fred in shirt with a stiff high collar,
an Edwardian style long past,
I with a hat I don't remember, and
a brooch I never owned.

It is a picture of my parents,
newly wed.

IN THE BEGINNING THERE WAS THE EGG

I like the way it nestles into my hand,
weightily, thoughtfully, smoothly,
before it all begins.

FALLOUT

Deposited,
I grew like a pearl,

bit of irritation
in God's eye.

Inside a tear
I splashed
to the ground.

Earthling, bonded, bound.

GOD, SPEAK TO ME

I wake up and pray:
God, please tell me what to do.
In the words of the radio preachers,
"Trust God and he will guide you."

Tucked under a comforter,
snuggled by a pillow on my right,
another on my left,
I wait.

Hours pass.
No answer.

I turn to priorities,
make a list,
repeat it like a litany
with the refrain,
God, please tell me what to do.

I hold my breath,
count to three, jump out of bed,
run to the medicine cabinet, take
methylenedioxymethamphetamine,

and I am off!

IN THE QUIET OF NIGHT

Relieved of time
I am a choir of voices
both pro and con
soon changed
to parrots' chatter
drowned out
by grating locust wings
dispersed
by roaming astral gales

then sleep affirms my one-ness
though not for long

LIFE MEASURED IN TIME

The animal instinct in us
does not know life ends.

Our human gift to measure
TIME— spoils it all.

No other animal wonders
what it will become

when it grows up—
not even tadpoles, or caterpillars.

II

SCARECROW

My body is a wooden cross
made of two broomsticks.
My head, a cranium, part skull, part helmet,
with a facial mask all welded in steel;
as is my meager shirt.
My hands are gardening gloves
stapled to my wrists.

Powerful and purposeful, I was happy
in the fields of Massachusetts.
The wind animated me,
rocked my outstretched arms in space,
bobbed my head into yeas and nays.
Creatures bolted, even dogs.

Now I stand by the door in a foyer,
stare past the ceiling, and dream
of being the loftiest of Icons
raised over a growing crowd
marching across Europe to deliver
Jerusalem from the infidel.

Until a door slams, and my head shifts
and I, helmeted guardian, watch
people come and go.

COMBAT

She stands behind a folding table
by the market's gate,
knife poised over a large fish

whose scales change color
with each gasping breath,
 from green to red to purple.

People stop to watch.
No customers step forward.

She grips the fish,
shoves it half, head first,
into a bag filled with water.

Revived,
it snaps its tail,
slaps her face.

She drops bag and fish.
Water rushes to the ground
from the table.

The fish now flicks its tail
with a force strong enough

to push deep into the sea,

instead the sound of fish
lashing wood
cuts through the air.

DOMINANCE

Two luminous green disks
hang midair in darkness.

My sight adjusts to a cat
sitting in majestic symmetry
on a tree trunk.

It has me in its gaze.
I stare at it,
narrow my eyes.

"Get lost! Scat!"
The "S" a missile,
the "T" an explosive,
knock it sideways,
as if hit by a rock.

IN DIFFERENT KEYS

First the room seems filled with drones,
then from within the din—
high-pitched sounds float to the ceiling.
The faster the pianist digs into the keys,
the more angelic voices he seems to free.

Somewhere in Arizona,
fingers play different keys,
launch a missile from a Drone.
With a high-pitched sound
the Hellfire rides to detonation.

Clouds of particles reach high into the sky,
three men walking along the Khyber Pass
are decimated.

FOR CENTURIES

The attacks are precise,
they come in waves.
The living run into gullies,
no structure escapes—
    twenty dwellings,
    twenty ruins.

Hamlet high in the mountains,
    where pathways
    are full of fragrance,
    fields terraced.

Forgotten amid larger objectives,
    anonymous farmers
    tend unnamed graves.

They know who died,
    not who is buried
    in which spot.
    Some graves
    have more than one body,
    or just unmatched parts.

Meanwhile oxen pull plows
    for the winter planting,
    and children
    harvest turnip leaves.

TSUNAMI

Finally, God showed his might,
Ruler of the Universe.

It went quickly,
it was soon over,
said a photographer
perched out of reach.

In ancient times, on this day
of triumph for the prophets,
people would have looked to
mend their ways.

It was hard to believe what I was seeing,
said a Norwegian looking for his wife,
a sea first draining, fish left flopping,
then a wall of water swallowed the earth whole!
Within minutes—all was gone.

We still hear them, see then, call them.
Near the fissures, life is forming,
while we mourn.

DIVINATION

Who shall live?
Who shall die?
Small bones fashioned
into dice on gaming tables
green like killing fields.

Hundreds of shovels
dig into Bosnian soil
uncover
enough bones to fill
millions of reliquaries.

A woman cries out,
"Bring me one bone of my son.
I will keep it on my pillow beside me,
at night."

WHAT WILL HE REMEMBER

In the fifth year of his life,
they filed through the back door
in the dark,
into the thunder of artillery,
past dead bodies
mauled by dogs—
step by step
to a thicket of dates
and orange trees,
down to the sandy edge
of the Euphrates.

Four boats to ferry hundreds—
one, a motor boat.

He will recall his siblings,
counting them on six fingers,
a name for each.

JUMP ROPE JINGLE

Death is my ally,
Death is my friend,
Death is my future,
Death is my end.

DARK REMEMBRANCE

The journey was a curse—
flights delayed for months,
visas not issued—
explosions shook buildings,
machine guns nattered.

People took turns standing in line
day and night,
waiting
for consulate doors to open.

In moonlight
they turned into ghosts—
a premonition.

NAZI GERMANY, WORLD WAR II

The smell of coffee in the morning,
the yellow of eggs,
bread with strawberry jam,
it could have gone on forever.

She was 18 years old,
could not denounce her friends,
chose execution.

Will history remember her?

EXECUTION

The witnesses jeer.
Saddam Hussein,
in a long gray coat,
shouts back:

*SO THAT'S
WHAT YOU HAVE ALL
BECOME!*

as the hooded hangman
slips the noose over his head,
and the trap door opens.

He lies dead,
head to one side.

The drop,
a momentary passage.

III

NONPAREIL

A guru put the Universe
into my lap,
spun me around with words
so fast,
the Universe and I
turned into one.

Imbued with cosmic spirit
my soul came free of fear,
I asked, "Guru,
where is the sense of humor
in this world?"

He fixed his gaze on me.
I laughed with my human voice
unique as God,
alone.

I FELL IN LOVE WITH A LION

Separated by a wire fence,
I looked lovingly into his beautiful
yellow eyes, rimmed with black.

He narrowed his gaze,
focused intensely,
hungrily.

Right from the start,
it did not go well.

WELLFLEET

When Angeline stirred the Francophile in you,
you serenaded her with French popular songs.

All the young mothers grew nervous,
like mares in a stall, nostrils flaring,
legs shifting. Their husbands grew jealous
of your fluency in French.

You wanted me to share your excitement
over another au-pair, here to learn English.

At five next morning
I stomped along the edge of the shore,
my feet razor-edged stencils in the sand.
I traced the arc of the sky to the horizon,
a yawning Leviathan, the sea
its palpitating tongue.
When it gathered more light in its jaws.
I veered inland, over the dunes, to the cottage.

You were drying your hair
with a brightly striped towel and said,
'aha' to my having watched daybreak,
while our toddlers banged their cereal spoons
in exuberant conversation.

VOICE MAIL

I got your message
but cannot comprehend it.
You're sorry you can't go to the Opera
Thursday. You are getting *engaged?*

For the last two weeks, I've been falling asleep,
night after night, to the rise and fall
of your mellow voice
engulfing me in the details of your life—
the first names of your mother, your father,
your sister, even that of your grandmother.

I even know what your childhood house
looked like, felt like, sounded like—
> the front door-bell, cranked by hand,
> made a rasping noise; your dog's nails
> clicking on the shellacked floors;
> your mother's voice from upstairs,
> "Is that you, Richard?"
> Your sister searching your room
> for secrets, love letters, girlie magazines;
> you reading her diaries in retaliation.
> The fishing trips with your father,
> who reeked of tobacco, and drunk gin
> from a shiny flask kept in his breast-pocket.

The boredom of it all, since he didn't talk,
and the fish never bit.
Your grandmother's wedding
to a third husband, so ossified,
he couldn't turn his head her way
to say "I do."

You changed your major
from ancient history to accounting.
But Opera is what you love, for its drama.
How happy you were to have found me
on the ticket line—
Where had I been all your life?

Don't you think, you should have
mentioned your fiancée, at least once?

IN TWO PLACES AT THE SAME TIME

What you say slips through my ears,
my mind busy with people you never knew.

All of us crowded into that convertible,
roof down, sun shining,
screaming with joy, because
life had just begun.

I hear you say, "Why don't you?"
Have no idea what it is about,
snap back, "Should I?"

MARS TO VENUS

He says,
"You calculating temptress, You!
Every move alluring—
I yearn for ecstasy
for boundaries to dissolve,
I the tiger,
I the prey."

"Turn the light out,"
she says.

VALENTINE

The message inside the envelope—

"Hope you roast in hell
next to your new lover!"

With a flick of my wrist
I light a match,
absolve the message.

YES

I spied you from my car.
How you have changed!
Your magnificent black mane
all gone.
What is your trademark now?

My life is a veritable orchard—
apples, cherries,
and the grass is sky high,
deep enough to lose a wedding ring.

Yes, I said *wedding ring*.

INTERLUDE

When you left, I watched the ship
become smaller and smaller
until it disappeared into the horizon,
off the globe, out of my life.

But the wind blew clouds
toward the harbor,
and in them I saw your silhouette.

How long will it take
before I stop talking to you?

YOU SHOULD HAVE BEEN THERE

I e-mail.
*So long, I'm off
to surrender to the unknown.*

The blank hospital wall
stares like the evil eye.

The anesthesiologist
asks: *What are you allergic to?*

Mostly life, I tell him,
in your absence.

SHE CALLS HIM HONEY

      burly and old,
smelling of decay,
his skin rippled like
the surface of a lake.

Honey!

Beeswax honeycombs come to mind,
each cell filled with sweetness,
suspended in gold,
the color of sunshine,

not the high pitched call
of the red-necked rooster
ordering the day into action,
like her husband
with his endless commands.

IV

POISON OAK

She wishes the poison oak
would die, fears
drops could splash back at her
when watering, or
children playing hide and seek
could lean against it.
She even keeps the dog indoors.

Her husband says,
he loves the poison oak—
gives life an edge,
keeps the marriage
from growing stale.

CIRCUS SCENE

Groom in tails
where is your whip
the show is starting
the show is starting

Here come the bridesmaids
in rows of three,
trotting on their dainty ankles,
curls flying,
ribbons floating.

Groom in tails
snap your whip
the bride is coming
the bride is coming

Fat flanks shaking,
a sturdy girth,
strong necked,
short legged,
she is prancing.

Groom in tails
Quick the ring
to loop the two of you
in marriage

Hurray! It's done.
Through the hoop she jumps—
the public steps into the arena,
to dance, to kiss, to feast, to sway.
Hurray, hurray, hurray, hurray!

Groom in tails
grasp your whip
jump on your bride
and gallop away

BALLAD

"My beloved, my beloved,
Screws others, screws others.
My beloved," says he,
"You can't do this to me."
To me!

"My beloved, my wife,
Mother of my child,
You can't do this
To your husband."
Your husband!

"Husband" says she,
"You can't husband yourself,
Let alone a wife and a child."
A child!

"You scream, and you shout,
You rant and you rave,
And malign us into the bargain."
The bargain!

"My beloved" says he,
"I will not pay your bills,
I will take the child
And you can walk the streets.
"*The streets!*

"My beloved, indeed!
I'm starved for love.
When did you last
Fondle me, my husband?"
My husband!

"My beloved, my beloved,
How can I make love
When you have touched others?"
Others!

"Please, please," screams the child,
"Don't rant and don't rave,
Make up
And love one another."
One another!

"Our sweet, our darling."
They coo, and coo,
And hug the child.
One trio, until their eyes meet.
Their eyes meet!

"Whore!" he shouts,
"Impotent bustard," she howls.
He grabs the child,
And she screeches "Mother!"
Mother!

"You motherfucker, you,"
 She yells out loud,
"What did your mother feed you
In her milk?"
Her milk!

"You bitch," barks he
And throws the child at her
Who sinks to the floor
In shambles.
In shambles!

The neighbors come running,
He lets them in,
With a gracious smile,
She asks, "Coffee?"
Coffee!

"Just playing, just playing"
They say flushed,
"Our little one has won.
Get up! You have won the game."
The game!

POST-MODERNISM

It was not gas,
it was a smile directed at me.

That this extension of self
gains consciousness,
becomes a vis-à-vis, who knows me,
adores me, depends on me,
turns to crawl and explore,
mine to catch and bring back,
and then send off to school,
to find her own forbidden fruit
and to say "Let go of me!
Stop telling me what to do!"

Rebellious, I think, grinning
to myself, until I discover
that she speaks a language
I do not know, and pursues
what I do not understand.

She pushes me out of the way
as if I were occupying a seat
not meant for me at my own table.

I love you, I love you—
It is I who decided to have you

"So what!? You fulfilled your need."

STEPMOTHER

I

In front of the pulpit
the new wife
turns to the boy,
slips a necklace over his head.

"With this locket
I promise you
from this day forward,
to be your mother,
to love and to cherish,
to care and to comfort,
in sickness and in health"

The twelve year old huddles in her arms,
the father embraces them both.

II

Now, she who promised,
speaks to him
in profile only.

In the park,
he wrenches a branch from a tree

brings it down full force
on a bench, again and again,
air whistling,
leaves shredding,
wood splintering,
until the branch breaks in two.

He hooks his hands under the bench,
turns it over with one thrust,
six legs jotting into space,
a felled beast.

He gouges handfuls of soil,
flings scalloped lumps
into the river,
feels sand under his nails,
feels it cuts into him
like her new-born twins,
his half-brothers.

Locket in hand
he wheels round, and round,
gains momentum,
lets go.

Amulet and chain
hurtle away,
disappear into the haze
of the Potomac River.

KEEP GOING

Driving, I see them in the rear-view mirror,
sitting side by side,
my sister and her ex-husband,
she radiant and animated,
he stifling a yawn.

An oncoming truck startles me,
piled high with dead cattle, melons,
uprooted fruit trees,
squawking geese tied to each other,
on top.

I swerve,
hit a boulder marked *50 Km*.

To where?

V

THE STINGING

A wasp blundered into my bedroom,
stung my upper arm.
I slapped it,
killed it, flicked it to the floor.

Later that night, in the hospital,
I signed a paper stating
I was aware
medicine is not a precise science.

The poison flowed through my veins.
Hives appeared on my thighs,
haunted me for weeks,

reminded me of another poison
stored in my veins,
since parenting
is not a precise science.

FATHER

My father in his signature bathrobe
watching boxing on TV,
twitches with every blow,
rolls his shoulders,
attacking, defending.
Self-made man,
he always plays both parts,
gravely disappointed
in his offspring.

DRUG RESISTANT

In my dream, large green leaves
sprout from the ceiling,
the size of elephant ears.
I watch them spread.

Silently they invade my space,
groomed and pampered.
They reach for me.
I don't want to be trapped
in a bower of leaves.

I call my doctor.
The pills are Valium,
he says.

My mother is on Valium.
I wrap the bottle,
mail it to her
three thousand miles away.

MOTHER

I am grown up now
and I don't remember you.
Where were you when I was a child?

That heavy female who walked through
my room sometimes,
was that you?

My children who love me,
hate me, and tease me,
are of me, and they know it.
Was I of you?

You could have been the shade
to a burning sun,
the light at the end of a dark hallway,
the answer to a question.

YOU CAN'T GO HOME AGAIN

After visiting with my mother
for several months,
my two-year-old son and I
are seen off,
kissed good bye,
seated in the plane.

The flight is canceled.
We return to my mother.

The crib has been dismantled,
my bed stripped,
windows wide open.

We sit in the kitchen,
homeless.

REVELATION

As a child, I loved you,
I pity you now,
her father says,
disapproving of her life style.

She shrugs,
old enough to be on her own,
sure enough
to stand next to him by the window,
look at the same view,
and see it differently.

It will be a long pause
before either one of them
says anything;
having nothing in common
but their genes.

WHEN WAS I THIS ALONE WITH ANYONE

    We felt the burden of your presence
        in your well-cut jacket
        that had to be hung just so.

    We tiptoed in the absence
        of your conversation,
        because you had to unwind
        in the stifled atmosphere
        of your demands.

    When you finally deigned to join us,
        you darkened the light
        with prophecies of our doom.

KID SISTER

She is our guest.
She has blossomed.
My spouse dotes on her,
my young son adores her,
our friends' husbands
pursue her.

Unadorned, she shines,
she moves gracefully,
life favors her.

When will she leave?
When will she age?

QUADRILLE

Between the hatred,
the bitterness,
the disappointments,
I am alive—
weave in and out,
stand sideways,
avoid collision.
Bypassed,
I veer around.

One partner
in this endless quadrille.

CAN YOU HEAR ME?

I don't know how to speak to you
when you are your other self,
removed from meaning,
turned inward.

My voice drowns in an empty space.
I string words into nonsense
to test your hearing,

while you scurry back and forth
in my line of vision
as if you needed a witness
to your plight.

Were you a fish,
I'd reel you in.

WRITER'S BLOCK

Bell without clapper
Dry mouth
Lame hand
Doors open
Close without rhythm
Slippered steps
Muffled thoughts
Eyes follow
Bluebottle up the wall
Upside-down on the ceiling

Will it fly

TIME ENTRAPPED

In a small square leather box,
a round dial
with stops,
no numbers,
wedged
between the four corners
of its world.

Best of all,
I can lock the box,
balance it on the palm of my hand
and feel bigger than Time.

VI

AFRICAN GOOD LUCK CHARM

Her long black hair like a mantilla
frames a dress made of pinhead-colored
beads strung into rows
of tiny pyramids.

With red double beads for each eye,
she looks astonished to fit so comfortably
into the grip of my hand.

ETRUSCAN OIL LAMP

This tiny round burner,
two inches in diameter,
cannot light a room, or a thought,
but multiplied by many, it can emblazon
a footpath to the road of enlightenment,
a hop and a skip in geological time.

MUSEUM, NY

A 4x5 patio flagstone mosaic
framed by pebbles,
Rome, circa 383 AD,
makes me stoop, touch the past.

Lucilius, age eleven,
saddles his pony;
little sister Theodora
sprinkles birdseeds
on the patio's tiles.

Meanwhile, their father,
Emperor Magnus Maximus
marches his Roman Legions
through Britain, Gaul, and Spain.

The museum guard taps me
on the shoulder,
Not permitted to touch!
he says, in his Haitian lilt.

PIERRE BONNARD: LARGE YELLOW NUDE

Why is she nude, in high heels,
facing a mirror without an image?
The length of her body— no frontal view—
bathed in yellow on yellow,
golden, undulating, organic,
a sensual pleasure to behold.

But does she see herself?

"THE HUNGRY GOD"
(Centerpiece at an exhibition, Beijing 2006)

Stripped chunk of tree trunk on doglike legs,
with wooden head of a pig, snout lifted skyward,
thin stick for tail points downward,
extended phallus parallels underbelly.

Mounted on a wooden plank,
the idol seems to plead for wheels and cord
to be pulled away.

AVANT-GARDE

The Avant-Garde
Resists
Mainstream
Ideology
With
PerformancePoetry
DisembodiedParlance
LifeAndArt
AreOne
YouAndI
ArePoets
WeSwimIn
Aesthetic
Populism
TheTriumph
OfMass
Communication
Over
TheWritten
Word
TheCentrists
Hostile
ToChange
DelayUs

Talk
NotAsThe
Crow
Flies
ButAsThe
Mind
Randomly
Palpitates
Words
IntoThe
Microphone

You'reOn
Go!

THE COLOR BLACK

Black was associated with sorrow,
with mourning, with death,
with evil, with ignorance, with night.

Now we squint to see black on black
in museums, in galleries.

Can you tell the many nuances
finally given full recognition?

BETRAYED

I dreamt I was airborne in a cocoon,
rocked by gentle winds,
when a twister flung me to the ground.

The cocoon split open.
Lush trees sheltered me,
sun rays reached out to warm me,
nature's low hum embraced me.

A rush of joy made me right myself,
try my insect wings,
but I keeled over. Dry leaves trembled
not from my weight, but from the tread
of a fast approaching chicken,
in a glorious red feather pelt,
with yellow-banded legs.

Love permeated me when
the chicken rolled me over.
Still not able to get up, it took me firmly
in its beak and raised me skyward.

I was ready to fly
when it swallowed me.

APERTURE

The discovery of the keyhole is a thrill
in everyone's life,
making doors transparent,
allowing the eye to view hidden worlds.

What untold revelations
before the unexpected condemnation
of being a spy, a peeping tom, a sinner,
two and half feet tall.

VII

TRAGICOMEDY

I loved to watch
sad sack Pierrot
run with mincing steps
and trembling knees
across a wire strung high
between two buildings,
staying aloft
by hanging on
for dear life,
to a mere balancing pole.

MOEBIUS-STRIP REALITY

I rush to the bank,
stand in line.
The clerks work
leaden-handed, nearsighted,
with a can't-be-rushed
meticulousness.

An explosion makes us duck.
A gigantic German shepherd sails
through a plate glass window,
continues over-head,
out the other side.
Sheets of shattered glass crash
noiselessly to the floor.

*This damn bank can't even keep
its customers safe!
The fricking police should keep
its dogs leashed!
Have you ever!
Some missile!*

My alarm clock goes off.
I rush to the bank,
stand in line.

The clerks work
leaden-handed, near-sighted,
with a can't be rushed
meticulousness.

ALTERNATE PARKING PRAYER

Please let me dive on eagle wings
to best the Romans at their game—
enmesh my silver steed
in their ordinance.

I see them from high above approaching
in pairs from East and West.
With throbbing heart I descend, key in hand.

Two in blue, and two in brown,
they pass each other poker faced.
Saved! No ticket.

ENCOUNTER

With a will of its own
a parked car
starts its backward descent
down a city street.

"Do something!" I shout
at a ragged man
coming up the hill.

"Me?" he asks surprised,
"but you've got to be my witness!"
Sliding behind the steering wheel
he stops the rolling car.

We grin at each other.
His eyes have come alive.

OLD-FASHIONED HERO

My first and last line
of defense is ordinariness.
In between,

I ride a white steed,
wear spurs and helmet,
wield a well honed sword.

Beware! I shout,
Save your head
from rolling in the dust.

This said, I'm back,
toeing the line.

FOLLOW YOUR DREAM

I ought to be
A swan that honks
Not a quacking duck

I really ought
To steer a ship
Not paddle a canoe

Or fly a transport plane
Not float a pink balloon

THE ROPE ARCHES HIGH

Two girls twirling a rope,
their teammates on opposite sides

A *one, a two, a three, a four...*

In they run under the rope,
leap four times, and out unscathed.

I sway back and forth
A *one, a two, a three, a four...*

The rope on down hits the ground,
I have my cue— in I leap,

A *one, a two, a three, a four...*

My body knows just what to do
I clear four score and ten, and out.

SOMEWHERE

I cross the border.
The sky is gray like a mare's belly,
water breaks, pelting the windshield.
I pull over, straining to see.
Ahead of me a rickety farmhouse.
I inch up to it.

Inside, four tables set for two.
Not a soul around.
Outside, miles of Canadian prairie.

Explosion after explosion,
thunder rolls off into the distance.
I stand by the window, watch
zigzagging electric charges
hit the prairie.

When I sit down, a waitress appears.
Before taking my order, she asks me to
write my name on a paper napkin ring.

Gladly!

PROTECTOR OF THE FAMILY

High in the Andean mountains,
guarding his fields,
he sits proudly
in his red jacket
trimmed with white.
A sombrero
shades his face,
wife by his side,
child on her arm,
and against his shoulder,
held by the crook of his left arm,
leans not a rifle,
but a double barreled flute.

VIII

THE KEY

Keys come in many shapes
for different locks,
but their task remains the same,
lock or unlock,
guard or reveal.

The key on the Costa del Sol
unlocks a back door
opening on a wide beach
with flocks of strutting pink flamingos,
their S shaped necks
an interlocking pattern
across a setting full moon
sinking into the sea.

CONVIVENCIA
(Spain 1252, Period of Accommodation)

When Don Carlos wants to learn Arabic,
he buys himself a household slave.

Mahmoud teaches him well.
The two men like each other
until Don Carlos hears
that in a crap game, Mahmoud
has cursed the Lord.

He beats him mercilessly.
Mahmoud stabs him.

Incarcerated, Mahmoud waits
for Court to convene.

Don Carlos goes to church
every day, prays for guidance,
wants Mahmoud punished,
not executed.

Mahmoud hangs himself.

Don Carlos thanks God the Just,
the Merciful, for His guidance.

POLITICALLY CORRECT IN ANOTHER ERA

Ten thousand thoughts crisscross the day
leaving no tangible trace.

The mindful, in search for more,
envision angels and demons
in heaven and hell,
ignoring their creative thoughts
for fear of being declared insane.

THE RIGHT TO LIFE AND THE PURSUIT OF HAPPINESS

Kicked out by his father like a cur,
he did what a dog can't do,
vandalized his parents' home,
took a ferry to Tangier.

Doorways, alleys, courtyards
find him sleeping, dreaming.
A crowd of people walking at a clip
turns into a horse stampede,
on whose backs he runs barefoot
counter to the surging horde;
comes across three people playing
chess, in costume.
Knows next to the Bishop stands the Queen,
that the hooded hangman is King.
He cracks his knuckles for good luck.
Enraged the hangman shouts,
"Open your mouth and reveal yourself!"
He opens his mouth wide,
wakes up hungry.

Begging, stealing, he drifts
until a hovel anchors him.
Nights wake him to pitch pennies

at a beach café,
where applauded, plied with drinks
he endures till morning,
staggers home to one more drink,
and nowhereness.

A sleeping life excites him.

THE WORLD IN THE PALM OF HER HAND

A sky-blue enameled cell phone
opens, closes with a muted click—
an object d'art,

gift from her abuelo
two months ago,
for coming of age at eighteen,
in New York City.

Use it to make yourself known,
he says, cupping her chin,
his eyes as luminous as hers.
She will raise them all
out of their poverty.

On her way to a college interview
clutching her resumé,
she hears the train approaching,
shifts the envelope from right to left.
The cell phone escapes her grip,
plummets to the tracks.

Gabriela, swift as a gazelle,
dives after it.
The sky-blue enamel back in her hand,
a collective shriek stops mid-air.

SURFING

I ride the surf
afraid to slip
into another sea
where raving waves beach
passion, guilt, and shame
on the seashore of the mind.

MISCAST

At 500 lbs., trapped in her flesh, bed-ridden,
food only can relieve the plight of her existence,
heal the broken symbiosis with her mother,
keep her in a state of one-with-nature.

One doctor tells her she will die soon,
another offers to wire her jaws shut,
a third one to remove 7 miles of intestines,
yet another tells her that she must hope
to be reborn.

Had I only been a tree, a banyan tree
held sacred for my spreading mass,
admired for my sprouting aerial roots,
all outcasts could have flocked to me for shelter
from sun, or rain, or night.

MISTAKEN COMMUNION

When asked on TV
what he feels,
serial killer Dahmer says:
Happy it is over.

His father, glad to see him
safe, assures us
Jeffrey was a normal child—
found petrified shin-bones,
twirled them like a drum majorette,
called them fiddle sticks,
explored insects and birds—
morbid curiosity, but not unusual.

Could we talk about homosexuality?
Asks the interviewer.
It's a sin, says pop.

Dahmer liked young men,
wanted them to stay on a little longer:
he loved them,
killed them,
dismembered them,
kept a limb or two as mementos,
incorporated others,
made them part of himself.

GODDESS OF BEEF CATTLE

She is the foremost authority
on animal care.

She says she understands them,
    sees what they see,
    hears what they hear.
Her emotions are simple,
the main one is fear.

She redesigned the dip-vat,
    replaced the slippery slide
    with a grooved ramp
    jutting out over water,
    tromp d'oeil only.
    The animals walk with confidence,
    fall in.
She calls it "Cattle walking on water."

She built curves into the road
from van to slaughterhouse,
illusions of short distances
free of prodding cowboys.

With every turn the road narrows
until, transformed, it rises

into conveyor rails
supporting underbelly,
legs dangling.

In close proximity,
comfortingly nose to rump,
like walking in a pasture, single file,
they ride up to the slaughter corridor,
to a bolt to the head that stuns them.

"Stairway to Heaven," she calls it.

Humane handling of cattle improves
the quality of meat.

GUEST CABIN

I lie down on a Danish recliner for the night,
facing a window overlooking a thicket
of pine trees behind the deck.

Attracting moths and gnats with my flashlight
in the dark, I glimpse a sliver of the moon
peek through the tree tops.

When moon light travels up my outstretched legs
I open my pocket mirror—
two polished rounds, hinged together.

A small full moon caught by one surface
reflected by the other, and with these two
tiny full moons in my hand, I fall asleep.

END OF SEASON

White sheets cover
the furniture in the house.
I am ready to leave.

Why are the bees hurling themselves
against the window panes?
The pool has turned into a lake
and laps at the front door.
A wooden rowboat
lies in wait.

The sound of creaking oars
makes me think of fishermen
setting out at dawn.

I row all day.
Blisters on the palms of my hands
inflate, open.

Flat as a coin
the planet spins between its poles,
and I with it.

IRRETRIEVABLE LOSSES

I am peering through lace,
each loop another life,
    suddenly fading.
I stagger—
    unsure of my destination.

Road signs gone,
well trodden paths obliterated.
the sun, the moon are there,
    but far away.

A new geography,
mountains, now valleys,
valleys, now lakes,
voices silenced.

I linger,
    let memories dominate,
    eyes closed to the vortex of time.

METAMORPHOSIS

When she fell sick
they came to tell her
that she would soon be well.

When she became worse
they assured her
that she would get better.

When she lingered
their eyes glazed,

they told her
of their daily activities,
then stopped coming.

Years later, when they heard
she was still alive,
they were startled.

SUBTERRANEAN ENCOUNTER

A tear in my dish towel
reminds me of the wash
left in the laundry room.

I rush through a maze
of steel gray corridors
to the sub-basement, where

in doeskin scuffs and striped
pajamas, my late father-in-law
stands perfectly at ease.

I live here now, he says.
Pleased, I nod, recalling

the steep descent into the catacombs
beneath the church in Vienna,
where iron cauldrons house royalty.

IX

NOT YET

Too painful to accept
Liora is gone
and we move on
waving goodbye
still turned
towards her
until distance
is big enough
to face away

THE WRITING ON THE WALL
(Dream Sequence)

My friend Tuck visits.
We walk to a French restaurant.
She enters, sits at a round table.
I stay behind, watch through the window.

She removes her hat,
looks at her shadow on the wall
as if it were a mirror,
shows the waiter how she wants her hair shaped.

I enter, walk past her,
down into the cellar
where doors are numbered
like days in a calendar.
I open one.

A jumble of decaying branches
fill the space,
push through the walls
into adjacent rooms.

Upstairs, Tuck sits now on a narrow bench
near the cashier,
beckons the Maître D'.

Shouldn't I have your phone number?
she asks,
*so my husband can make reservations
after I'm gone?*

He shakes his head.

BEGUILED

I heard your hurried steps approach,
nude, but for red suede slippers,
a crystal necklace, bead for bead,
around your neck, past collar bones,
curved just below your throat,
matched by drop earrings,
short of shoulder length.

Your vitreous luster
made me sit up, surprised,
Where did you get all these?

Smiles changed to laughter,
unfurled like magic paper flowers,
burst into vibrating guffaws.

Beyond you, I spied our corridor
sneak past framed remains
of many years—
portraits of your parents and mine,
a bright-eyed you in uniform,
I, age 5, in ballet dress,
our children growing up.

Secluded in our privacy,

I forgot my good-byes
in the hospital room
where early morning stubbles
on your cheeks did not speak
of another day.

FREE ZONE

From the bus up Broadway
I saw sculptured trees—
crowns trimmed into cubes and cones.

Look, I exclaimed, my elbow jabbing
my late husband's ribs,
this can't be the #104.
The passengers in the bus
bantered and laughed,
as if they knew us.

Everybody got off the bus
at a station marked
FREE ZONE

We walked single file
between gray, dusty mounds
to higher grounds, and squatted
in a circle with the rest of the lot.

Over there, said a young man
pointing at a market stall,
is an excellent place for mementos.
Brown and black leather

body bags dangled from the ceiling.

A *bazaar*, I shouted joyfully,
and froze.

COMMEMORATION

I heard you drifted into
mindless darkness again
on your son's memorial day.

When you see him now,
is his wife with him?
He 34 and she 29, forever,
dead by choice.

A Mexican birthday table for the dead,
seems right to prepare for them,
 with sweets and cakes,
in the shape of skulls and skeletons.

Then you ought to rise and dance
in a black body stocking,
face whitened with chalk,
mouth crimson from ear to ear,
eyebrows traced into arches
of permanent surprise;
with empty tin cans strung around
your waist, tied to wrists and ankles,
so they can swing and clank,
and scrape the floor.

Dance!

Dance your pain in shoes with cleats
that hammer into the floor
truths lips can't frame, or screams relieve,
until you drop.

BRINGING YOU UP TO DATE

We lie side by side,
in the dark,
all partitions removed.
I know your thoughts
and you know mine.

Still, I bring you up to date
as if time mattered,
even in this seamless moment.

I tell you about the internet,
the Soviet Empire, now splintered,
Germany reunited,
the century turned.

It is not because you don't believe me
that you are gone
when dawn dissolves
the night.

LUCK, MY HEATHEN GOD

How could you let me fall prey
to forces that dim my eyesight?

You used to hover
near me. I reached for you,
pulled you close,
whispered—*please,*
and you protected me.

Couldn't you have warned me,
like the blinking lights
in department stores
signal me to exit
before it all goes dark?

ALTERNATE UNIVERSE

It says *Open*.
I climb through the O
into a walled yard.

I have erred.
The O is not for Open,
but for zero.

A mathematician told me
equations resulting in zero
speak of stability, while
between zero and one
there are endless possibilities.

All I want is to exit.
Where is the O for *Out*?

ABOUT THE AUTHOR

Mary Himmelweit, who speaks four languages and can communicate in four more, finds poetry the perfect medium to make a long story short. She studied economics and behavioral psychology, taught English as a Second Language, and welded steel sculptures. She lives in New York City and has a son and a daughter.

www.ingramcontent.com/pod-product-compliance
Lightning Source LLC
Chambersburg PA
CBHW051807040426
42446CB00007B/566